ARE WE THERE YET?

ALL ABOUT THE PLANET SATURN!
SPACE FOR KIDS

Children's Aeronautics & Space Book

D1737423

BABY PROFESSOR

EDUCATION KIDS

Speedy Publishing LLC
40 E. Main St. #1156
Newark, DE 19711
www.speedypublishing.com

Saturn is the sixth planet in the Solar system.

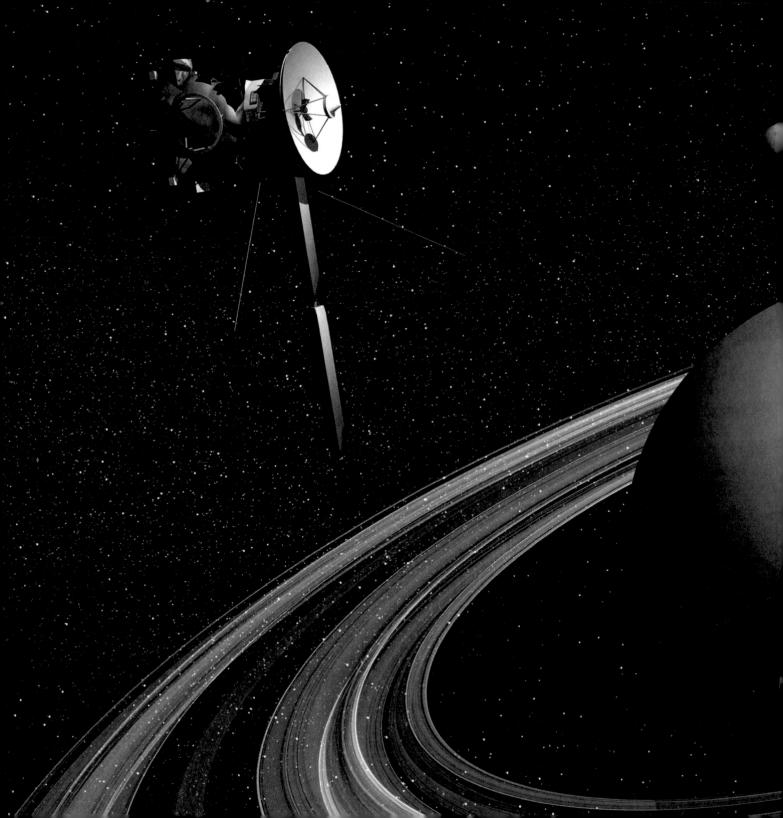

Saturn is the 2nd biggest planet in our solar system.

Saturn is also the lightest planet in our Solar System.

If there is a tub big enough to hold Saturn, it will just float in the water.

The distance of Saturn from the Sun is approximately 856 million miles.

Saturn is surrounded by a system of rings. The rings are 169,800 miles wide.

The rings
are made up
of particles
of ice, dust
and rocks.

The rings were discovered by Galileo Galilei in 1610 through a telescope.

Saturn is composed of hydrogen and helium.

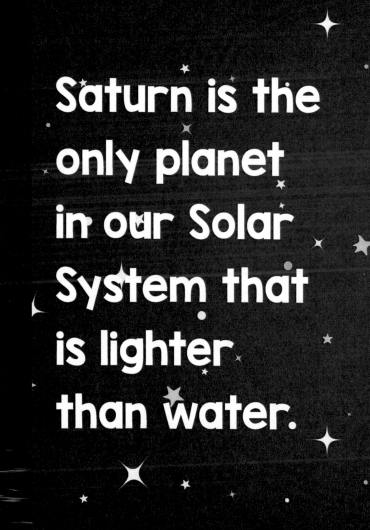

Saturn is the only planet in our Solar System that is lighter than water.

The diameter of Saturn is approximately 120,000 kilometers.

It takes
Saturn 29
and 1/2
years to
complete 1
revolution
around
the Sun.

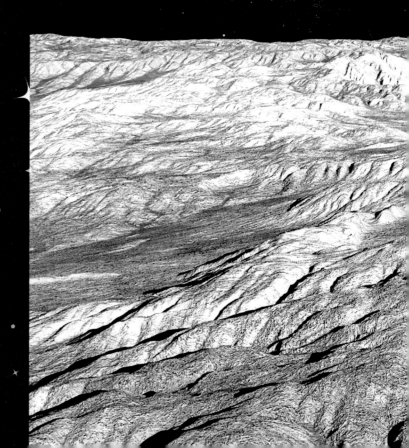

Saturn has 62 confirmed moons. 53 of them have names.

Titan is the largest moon of Saturn and the second largest moon in our solar system.

The distance
to Saturn
from Earth
is around
746 million
miles.

Saturn's temperature is believed to be around -270 degrees Fahrenheit.

Saturn completes a full rotation in just about 10 hours.

Saturn's rings orbit at different speeds and have gaps between them.

Saturn is
the furthest
planet that
can be seen
with just the
naked eye.

31027457R00024

Made in the USA
San Bernardino, CA
01 April 2019